CW00347380

Wrocław Travel Highlights

Best Attractions & Experiences

Donald Harris

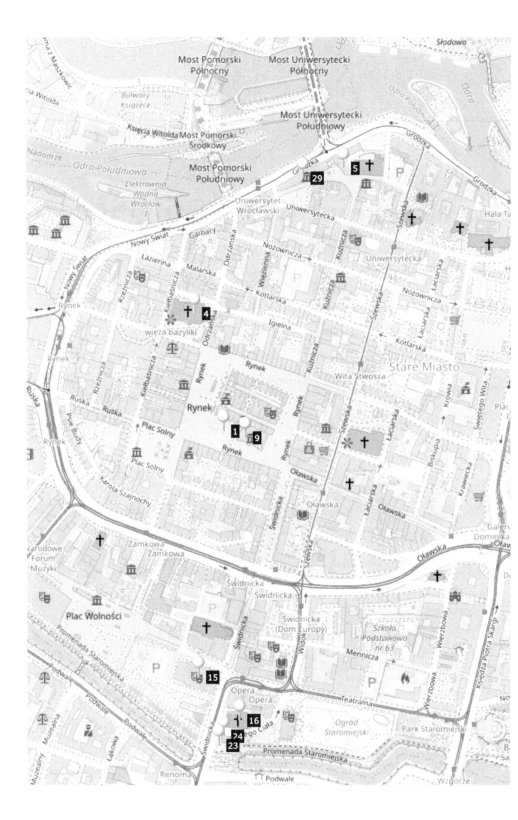

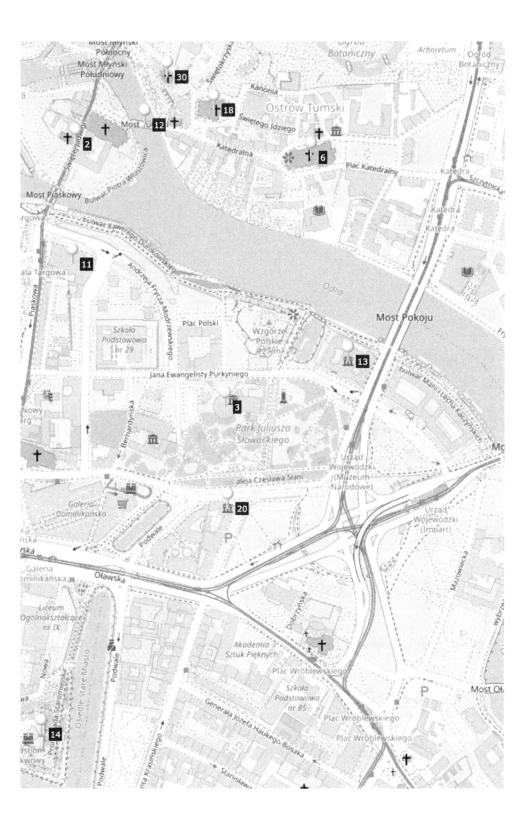

Contents

Welcome to Wrocław

The historic Wrocław is a city in western Poland, in the southeastern part of Lower Silesia. In June 2007, the city became the World Capital of Culture.

Wrocław is home to Centennial Hall, an UNESCO World Heritage Site featuring a Panorama of Racławice, a 360° oil painting that offers a panoramic view of a historic battle fought near Wrocław. The city also features a scenic Market Square (Rynek).

☐ 1. Market Square

Address: 1 Rynek Ratusz, Wrocław 50-106, Poland

The Market Square in Wrocław is a historical place surrounded with buildings in different styles. Its most recognizable landmark is the town hall standing at its center. A few hundred years ago the square hosted Wrocław's biggest market, which was famous all over Europe. On this site, merchants from the whole continent met to trade their goods. The Market Square has also witnessed many significant events in Polish history, especially during World War II when it served as a place for German army parades and Nazi propaganda demonstrations.

☐ 2. Cathedral Island

Address: 13 Świętej Jadwigi, Wrocław 50-266, Poland

Walk through the narrow lanes of Wroclaw, Poland's fourth largest city, to become fascinated by its history. The heart of this ancient city is its renowned Market Square with St Elizabeth's Church and St Nicholas's Church facing each other. The Vistula river brings even more grandeur to this location. When visiting this beautiful Polish city you can't miss out on some of the oldest architecture, including Wroclaw Town Hall, Ostrów Tumski - Bishop's Island with the All Saints' Church and the former Jesuits' College located there.

☐ 3. Racławice Panorama

Address: Jana Ewangelisty Purkyniego 11, 53-110 Wrocław, Poland
Phone: +48 71 344 16 61
Email: biuro@panoramaraclawicka.pl
Web: https://panoramaraclawicka.pl/

Walk through this painting and see the Battle of Racławice

unfold in one circular motion. Made in 1891, the Racławice Panorama is one of only a few preserved relics of a genre of 19th-century mass culture. The view begins with the battle scene and opens out onto the surrounding landscape. See plumes of smoke rise from burning ammunition depots, portraits representing famous individuals who contributed to the fight, and an original soundtrack that makes you feel like you're in the 19th-century.

□ 4. St. Elisabeth's Church

Address: świętej Elżbiety 3, 53-110 Wrocław, Poland

Phone: +48 71 343 72 04

Web: http://elzbieta.org/

St. Elizabeth's Church is a Gothic church in Wroclaw. It was placed under the care of the Catholic Third Order of Saint Francis. The church was placed on the list of monuments at the end of the 20 century for its historical significance and architectural value.   In 1993, it became a historical monument.

□ 5. Aula Leopoldina

Address: Plac Uniwersytecki 1, 53-110 Wrocław, Poland
Phone: +48 71 375 22 45

Aula Leopoldina in Wrocław is one of the most lavish baroque ceiling's ever created. Constructed in 1702-4 by Italian architect Giovanni Battista Tiepolo it is located within the Collegium Maius (Main College), the oldest building of the Wrocław University.

□ 6. Wrocław Cathedral

Address: 18 Plac Katedralny, Wrocław 50-329, Poland

The Wrocław Cathedral, Wrocław, is the seat of the Roman Catholic Archdiocese of Wrocław and a landmark of the city of Wrocław. The cathedral, located in the Ostrów Tumski district, is a Gothic church with Neo-Gothic additions. The current standing cathedral is the fourth church to have been built on the site.

□ 7. Wrocław Fountain

Address: Aleja Dąbska 1, 53-110 Wrocław, Poland

Email: info@wroclawskafontanna.pl

Web: http://www.wroclawskafontanna.pl/

The multimedia Wrocław Fountain is situated at the foot of the Sola Street in Wrocław's historical market square, and overlooks Saint Martin's Church. It was designed by Polish architect Józef Gosławski. The fountain has an oval pond of 41.5 x 78 m (135 x 256 ft) with flora and decorative fountains, which are placed in the four corners of the pond. The main fountain is located at the center of the pond, while two smaller additional fountains are located on both ends of the pond.

☐ 8. Centennial Hall

Address: Zygmunta Wróblewskiego 1, 53-110 Wrocław, Poland
Phone: +48713475150
Web: http://www.halastulecia.pl/

Centennial Hall, formerly named Hala Ludowa, is a historic building in Wrocław. It was constructed according to the plans of architect Max Berg in 1911–1913, when the city was part of the German Empire. Max Berg designed Centennial Hall to serve as a multifunctional structure to host 'exhibitions, concerts, theatrical and opera performances, and sporting events.' The hall continues to showcase everything from religious masses to circuses over its 111-year history.

□ 9. Wrocław Town Hall

Address: 20 Rynek, Wrocław 50-101, Poland
Web: http://maximus38.flog.pl/wpis/12418444

The Old Town Hall of Wrocław is one of Poland's most important historical landmarks. The original Gothic town hall stood at the center of the old market square until 1405. It was destroyed by the Hussites. After it was rebuilt, it served as a prison for many years, taking on an ominous reputation. Today, the Old Town Hall houses the offices of the mayor of Wroclaw, as well as features ceremonial rooms that are often used for exhibitions and civic events. Its interesting architecture inspires photographers to capture its stunning details.

☐ 10. Wrocław Zoological Garden

Address: Wróblewskiego 1-5 51-618, Wrocław, Poland
Phone: +48 71 348 30 24
Email: lutra@zoo.wroc.pl
Web: http://zoo.wroclaw.pl/

The Wrocław Zoological Garden has over 1100 species of animals, including 2 species of apes (gorilla and chimpanzee) and 105 species of birds. It is the only zoo in Poland that keeps chimpanzees, three Asian elephants, zebras, pumas, Asian black bears, cheetahs, kangaroos and tapirs.

□ 11. Wrocław Market Hall

Wrocław Market Hall was designed by Richard Plüddemann and built between 1906-1908 as the Breslauer Markthalle Nr 1. Wrocław used to be known as Breslau in German and Płock in Polish during its inter-war years. It has been made a landmark edifice of the city's Polish history. It is an example of German Modern architecture in Poland and offers an experience that reveals how life in large Polish cities was turned upside down after World War I.

☐ 12. Tumski Bridge

Address: 2 Katedralna, Wrocław 50-328, Poland

Tumski Bridge is a steel bridge in Wroclaw, Poland. Constructed in 1889 it replaced an old wooden bridge to connect Ostrów Tumski and Wyspa Piaskowa.   Until 1945, its name was Dombrücke.   This Tramway Bridge is called Cathedral Bridge or Green Bridge. It is a place of frequented by local couples in love.

☐ 13. National Museum, Wrocław

Web: http://www.mnwr.art.pl/

The National Museum (Narodowe Muzeum) in Wrocław was established in 1948. It is one of the largest museum collections in Poland with over 600,000 works; contemporary art is presented in about 10% of these. The collections were connected with the history of border shifts as a result of the Second World War as well as with the incorporation into Poland's territory following the Yalta and Potsdam Agreements.

□ 14. Wzgórze Partyzantów

Address: 10 Nowa, Wrocław 50-082, Poland

The small Wzgórze Partyzantów, Wrocław (English: Hill of the Partisans) is located at Milicka St. in Wrocław. It's a small park with a sculpture in its middle. The building used to be the headquarters of the Polish Army, but now it is an Army Museum called "Wieża Cukrowni Ratuszowa" (English: Sugar Mill Ratuszowa Tower). Wzgórze Partyzantów is a friendly place with no cars, where you can relax.

◻ 15. Wrocław Opera

Phone: +48 71 370 88 50

Web: http://www.opera.wroclaw.pl/

The Wrocław Opera House was first opened in 1841 and up to 1945 was named after the city's former German name, Oper Breslau.

☐ 16. Corpus Christi Church

Address: 1 Bożego Ciała, Wrocław 50-051, Poland

Corpus Christi Church in Wrocław is a Gothic church with a wooden roof, located at the corner of Świdnicka and ul. Bożego Ciała. It is the largest timber-framed church in Poland and one of the largest of its kind in Europe. Its architecture dates from the beginning of the 14th century, when it was built as a single-nave basilica, to the 16th century, when side chapels and a polygonal vestry were added.

☐ 17. Japanese Garden

Address: ul. Mickiewicza, 51-618 Wrocław, Poland
Phone: +48 71 3286611
Web: https://www.ogrod-japonski.wroclaw.pl/

The Japanese Garden in Wrocław is one of the largest in Europe and the only one in Poland. It was founded in 1909–1913 as an exotic garden for an exhibition, but due to World War I, this never happened. Officially opening in 1922, it was designed by Antoni Jurasz after he visited local gardens in Japan. The garden has exhibits of plants native to various landscapes within Japan including mixed woodland, swampy pasture, alpine plants and evergreen forest.

☐ 18. Church of the Holy Cross & St. Bartholomew

Address: 1 Plac Kościelny, Wrocław 50-328, Poland

The Collegiate Church of the Holy Cross and St. Bartholomew is a two-storey brick Gothic church on the Cathedral Island, which lays within the Old Town district of Wrocław. It was initially constructed before 1346, but it's main baroque re-construction was completed in 1728. The church has many interesting features that include an astronomical clock, Baroque altarpieces, sculptures, 17th-18th century tombstones.

☐ 19. Grunwald Bridge

Address: Most Grunwaldzki, Wrocław 50-123, Poland

The Grunwald Bridge is a suspension bridge that spans the River Oder in Wrocław. The bridge was designed by architect Richard Plüddemann and was built between 1908–1910. Its main purpose was to connect the railway network of Germany and Prussia with Silesia and Galicia. The bridge was named after the nearby Battle of Grunwald (1410). There's a reconstruction of one artillery piece from this battle – Broken Spear – standing by the north side of the bridge.

☐ 20. Post and Telecommunications Museum

Address: 1 Zygmunta Krasińskiego, Wrocław 50-414, Poland
Web: https://www.muzeum.wroclaw.pl/

The Muzeum Poczty i Telekomunikacji (Post and Telecommunications Museum) has over 25,000 historical objects related to the history of postal service and telecommunications. Its exhibits include equipment used by couriers to deliver mail throughout the ages, telegraph machines, stamp collection, documents expositions, equipment that took part in the first long distance call between Warsaw and Poznan, wireless devices that sent the first message for broadcast live between Wrocław and Istanbul.

☐ 21. Municipal Stadium

Address: Al. Śląska 1, 54-118 Wrocław, Poland

Phone: +48 71 77 68 000

Email: biuro@2012.wroc.pl

Web: http://www.stadionwroclaw.pl/

The Municipal Stadium in Wroclaw is a UEFA Category Four stadium built for the 2012 UEFA European Football Championship. The Stadium is located on Aleja Slaskiego in the western district of Pilczyce. It is the home stadium of the Sleaslk Wroclaw football team playing in the Polish Ekstraklasa. During the 2012 UEFA Euros the city hosted two 1/8 matches and one quarter-final.

□ 22. Jewish Cemetery

Address: Ślężna 37/39, 53-110 Wrocław, Poland

The Wrocław Jewish Cemetery is the resting place for the great Breslau Jewish community. Especially worth seeing are the ornate tombstones. Every detail is perfectly carved and every relief is carefully polished. The combination of real gold with black stone looks impressive to this day.

☐ 23. Wrocław's dwarfs

Address: Świdnicka, Wrocław 50-068, Poland
Web: http://Wrocławs_dwarfs/

Around a thousand different types of Wrocław's dwarfs have been created since 2005. Each one has a name, and they come in various poses. All of them are made of ceramic, and some of them include various items such as hats, glasses, jackets and even cigarette holders. Thousands of tourists visit Wrocław every year to search for the dwarfs and take pictures with them.

□ 24. Galeria M Shopping Mall

Address: 36 Świdnicka, Wrocław 50-068, Poland

Web: http://www.galeriam.com/

Galeria M is a modern shopping gallery located within the Wroclaw city centre. The mall is situated right next to the Palace of Arts and covers about 14,000 m² of the total 17,500 m² of the building. Here you will find a variety of boutiques, eateries and entertainment options.

□ 25. Arkady Shopping Centre

Address: Ul. Powstańców Śląskich 2-4, 53-333 Wrocław, Poland

Phone: +48 71 776 11 22

Email: biuro@arkadywroclawskie.pl

Web: http://www.arkadywroclawskie.pl/

At the heart of one of Poland's most vibrant cities, Arkady Shopping Centre offers choice for everyone. For those who prefer browsing in shops, you'll discover around 110 different retail outlets. The centre has an impressive aquarium on its second floor, with framed glass panelling to give you great views. And if it's entertainment you're looking for, there are restaurants, a cinema and even a large bowling alley all within easy walking distance of the Centre.

☐ 26. Olympic Stadium

The Olympic Stadium in Wrocław is used mostly for American football—home of the Panthers Wrocław and speedway racing, it also serves as the home stadium of Sparta Wrocław.

The stadium is a classic example of interwar functionalism. The original capacity was 15,000, but stands were demolished after the Second World War and a cycling velodrome was built in its place. In 1976 a roof-covered terrace for stand spectators was erected on the stadium's western side, while a row of small floodlights were installed above the race track, allowing to stage speedway races there. The last renovation took place in 1998.

☐ 27. Museum of Natural History

Part of the University of Wroclaw, this highly popular museum is home to over 1.5 million items including displays mainly on entomology and palaeontology. Some other displays also feature other areas of zoology. The museum's insect collections include Friedrich Wilhelm Niepelt's collection of exotic butterflies, Johann Ludwig Christian Gravenhorst, Ichneumonidae, caddisflies and grasshoppers.

□ 28. Wrocław University of Science and Technology

Wrocław University of Science and Technology is a public research university was founded in 1945 as a "higher technical school". It has been awarded the European Logistics Association Charter for a logistics study program implemented at the Faculty of Technics and Management in October 2014.   In August 2015, the university was accepted into the European Universities Association.

□ 29. Mathematical Tower

Address: 7 Plac Uniwersytecki, Wrocław 50-137, Poland

The Wieża (Mathematical Tower) is part of the former complex of the Faculty of Mathematics and Computer Science at the

University of Wrocław.   It has 10 floors and was built in a hyperboloid shape.

□ 30. Kościół Świętego Marcina

Address: 10 Świętego Marcina, Wrocław 50-327, Poland

With its distinctive bell towers, the Kościół Świętego Marcina, Wrocław is an excellent example of Silesian Gothic architecture. Saint Martin's church was built in 14th century and underwent major reconstruction works in 16th century.   It is one of the most prominent religious monuments in Lower Silesia, with several services held there everyday.

□ 31. Wrocław University of Economics

Address: Wrocław 53, Poland

Wrocław University of Economics and Business (Polish: Wyższa Szkoła Ekonomiczna we Wrocławiu, abbreviated as WSEiW) is one of ten public universities located in Wrocław. Originally established as a private business school in 1947 as Wyższa Szkoła Handlowa we Wrocławiu, it soon became one of the leading institutions of higher education in Poland. In October 1974 the university was named after the famous Polish economist Oskar Lange.

□ 32. University of Environmental & Life Sciences

Address: 53 Grunwaldzka, Wrocław 50-357, Poland

The University of Environmental and Life Sciences in Wrocław is a public higher education institution founded in 1951 as Agricultural Academy. Nowadays the University is a leader among Polish public research universities, as well as one of the most acclaimed institutions in Europe – according to the Chinese Universities Ranking, UW was ranked as number 10 university in the region of Western Europe. The University has been rewarded over 27 million PLN by the National Science Centre for five years, for innovative research.

☐ 33. Hala Orbita

Hala Orbita is the multi-purpose indoor arena in Wrocław. It hosts the home games of Śląsk Wrocław, WKS Śląsk Forza Wrocław and Gwardia Wrocław. It has a seating capacity for 3500 people. It is used to host sport event like volleyball, handball, basketball, indoor football and gymnastics as well as venue for competitions of martial arts, concerts, artistic events, fairs, exhibitions and even trade shows.

Picture Credits

Wrocław, Poland Cover: pedro-wroclaw / 5062333 (Pixabay)
Market Square: Pundit (CC BY-SA 4.0)
Cathedral Island: Natalkax (PD)
Racławice Panorama: Barbara Maliszewska (CC BY-SA 3.0 pl)
St. Elisabeth's Church: Nicolaswrocek (CC BY-SA 2.0 fr)
Aula Leopoldina: Bazie (CC BY-SA 3.0 pl)
Wrocław Cathedral: Aw58 (CC BY-SA 3.0)
Wrocław Fountain: Rdrozd (GFDL)
Centennial Hall: Robert Niedźwiedzki (CC BY-SA 3.0)
Wrocław Town Hall: Vorwerk (PD)
Wrocław Zoological Garden: Andrzej Otrębski (CC BY-SA 3.0)
Wrocław Market Hall: Thyes (PD)
Tumski Bridge: Magnaj (CC BY-SA 3.0)
National Museum, Wrocław: Giovanni Santi (PD)
Wzgórze Partyzantów: Barbara Maliszewska (CC BY-SA 3.0 pl)
Wrocław Opera: Barbara Maliszewska (CC BY-SA 3.0 pl)
Corpus Christi Church: Bonio (CC BY 3.0)
Japanese Garden: Andrzej Otrębski (CC BY-SA 3.0)
Church of the Holy Cross & St. Bartholomew: Walek (CC BY-SA 3.0 pl)
Grunwald Bridge: Merlin (CC BY 2.5)
Post and Telecommunications Museum: Neo[Ezn] (CC BY-SA 3.0)
Municipal Stadium: Marcin Kubiś (CC BY-SA 3.0)
Jewish Cemetery: Aneta Hoppe (Kfas) (CC-BY-SA-3.0)
Wrocław's dwarfs: Pnapora (CC BY-SA 3.0)

Arkady Shopping Centre: (Wt-Shared) Drzymek (PD)

Olympic Stadium: Nobbip (PD)

Museum of Natural History: Klapi (CC BY-SA 3.0)

Wrocław University of Science and Technology: Jar.Ciurus (CC BY-SA 3.0 pl)

Kościół Świętego Marcina: Jan Onufry Zagłoba (CC BY 3.0)

University of Environmental & Life Sciences: Dobowet (CC-BY-SA-3.0)

Hala Orbita: Gajowy07 (CC BY-SA 4.0)

Printed in Great Britain
by Amazon

26636684R00030